W9-CLB-978

PERCENTAGE

Marsha Arvoy and Dorianne Nardi

Crabtree Publishing Company
www.crabtreebooks.com

Author: Marsha Arvoy and Dorianne Nardi
Publishing plan research and development:
  Sean Charlebois, Reagan Miller
  Crabtree Publishing Company
Editor: Molly Aloian
Editorial director: Kathy Middleton
Project coordinator: Margaret Salter
Prepress technician: Margaret Salter
Coordinating editor: Chester Fisher
Series editor: Jessica Cohn
Project manager: Kumar Kunal (Q2AMEDIA)
Art direction: Rahul Dhiman (Q2AMEDIA)
Cover design: Shruti Aggarwal (Q2AMEDIA)
Design: Kanika Kohli (Q2AMEDIA)
Photo research: Poloumi Basu (Q2AMEDIA)

Photographs:
Istockphoto: DNY59: front cover; Natalya Ivaniadze: title page, p. 19;
  Marek Mierzejewski: p. 14-15, 20; Bonnie Jacobs: p. 5, 21
Dreamstime: Albo: p. 7; Chris Lofty: p. 15 (middle, left)
Fotolia: Hoangthinguyet: p. 13
Shutterstock: Sharon Morris: p. 9; Olga Chernetskaya & Leonid Yastremsk;
  p. 11; FloridaStock: p. 15 (left); Doug Lemke: p. 15 (middle, right);
  Krzysztof Wiktor: p. 15 (right); Elena Elisseeva: p. 18
Big Stock Photo: Brenda Klinger: p. 17

Library and Archives Canada Cataloguing in Publication

Arvoy, Marsha
    Percentage / Marsha Arvoy & Dorianne Nardi.

(My path to math)
Includes index.
ISBN 978-0-7787-5246-2 (bound).--ISBN 978-0-7787-5293-6 (pbk.)

    1. Percentage--Juvenile literature. I. Nardi, Dorianne II. Title.
III. Series: My path to math

QA117.A78 2009   j513.2'45   C2009-905362-4

Library of Congress Cataloging-in-Publication Data

Arvoy, Marsha.
 Percentage / Marsha Arvoy & Dorianne Nardi.
   p. cm. -- (My path to math)
 Includes index.
 ISBN 978-0-7787-5246-2 (reinforced lib. bdg. : alk. paper) -- ISBN 978-0-7787-5293-6 (pbk. : alk. paper)
 1. Percentage--Juvenile literature. 2. Estimation theory--Juvenile literature. I. Nardi, Dorianne. II. Title. III. Series.

 QA117.A78 2010
 513.2'45--dc22
                                2009035494

Crabtree Publishing Company

Printed in China/122009/CT20090903

www.crabtreebooks.com   1-800-387-7650

Published in Canada
Crabtree Publishing
616 Welland Ave.
St. Catharines, ON
L2M 5V6

Published in the United States
Crabtree Publishing
PMB 59051
350 Fifth Avenue, 59ᵗʰ Floor
New York, New York 10118

Published in the United Kingdom
Crabtree Publishing
Maritime House
Basin Road North, Hove
BN41 1WR

Published in Australia
Crabtree Publishing
386 Mt. Alexander Rd.
Ascot Vale (Melbourne)
VIC 3032

Contents

A Visit to the Zoo

The day of the school trip has arrived. The school has four second-grade classes, with 25 students in each class. All four classes are going to the zoo!

Mr. Santiago takes attendance, and all students are present today. No one is away. This means that all 100 children are going on the trip. Another way to say that the whole group is going is to say that 100 **percent** of the group is going. The **symbol** for percent is %. We can write one hundred percent like this: 100%.

Activity Box

Can you think of a time when 100 percent of your class participated in an activity?

This chart represents all the children. All 100 boxes are filled in. ▶

1	11	21	31	41	51	61	71	81	91
2	12	22	32	42	52	62	72	82	92
3	13	23	33	43	53	63	73	83	93
4	14	24	34	44	54	64	74	84	94
5	15	25	35	45	55	65	75	85	95
6	16	26	36	46	56	66	76	86	96
7	17	27	37	47	57	67	77	87	97
8	18	28	38	48	58	68	78	88	98
9	19	29	39	49	59	69	79	89	99
10	20	30	40	50	60	70	80	90	100

The students will not go to class today. They will go to the zoo!

What Is Percent?

Two buses take the children to the zoo. Each bus holds 50 children. This means that 50 of the 100 children ride on one bus, and the other 50 children ride on the other bus.

Each bus has 50 out of 100 children, or 50% of the children.

The word percent means "per one hundred" or "out of 100." A percent represents a part of 100.

Activity Box

If 50 out of 100 students are boys, what percent is that?

Each bus takes half,
or 50% of the students.

1	11	21	31	41	51	61	71	81	91
2	12	22	32	42	52	62	72	82	92
3	13	23	33	43	53	63	73	83	93
4	14	24	34	44	54	64	74	84	94
5	15	25	35	45	55	65	75	85	95
6	16	26	36	46	56	66	76	86	96
7	17	27	37	47	57	67	77	87	97
8	18	28	38	48	58	68	78	88	98
9	19	29	39	49	59	69	79	89	99
10	20	30	40	50	60	70	80	90	100

▲
50 students
on 1st bus

▲
50 students
on 2nd bus

Twenty-Five Percent

The children arrive at the zoo. Out of 100 children, 25 percent of the 100 students want to visit the monkeys first. The rest of the students want to see the gorillas.

When we say 25 percent of the students, we mean 25 out of 100 students want to visit the monkeys.

1	11	21	31	41	51	61	71	81	91
2	12	22	32	42	52	62	72	82	92
3	13	23	33	43	53	63	73	83	93
4	14	24	34	44	54	64	74	84	94
5	15	25	35	45	55	65	75	85	95
6	16	26	36	46	56	66	76	86	96
7	17	27	37	47	57	67	77	87	97
8	18	28	38	48	58	68	78	88	98
9	19	29	39	49	59	69	79	89	99
10	20	30	40	50	60	70	80	90	100

▲ Twenty-five percent of students want to see the monkeys first.

Activity Box

The red section on the number chart above shows that 25 percent of the students want to visit the monkeys. If 75 out of 100 children want to visit the gorillas, what percent is that?

A larger percent of the children want to see the gorillas first. A smaller percent wish to visit the monkeys.

Seventy-Five Percent

After visiting the monkeys and gorillas, the children meet up again. Out of 100 children, 75 percent choose to visit the reptile house next. The rest go to see the sea lions. It is the sea lions' feeding time.

1	11	21	31	41	51	61	71	81	91
2	12	22	32	42	52	62	72	82	92
3	13	23	33	43	53	63	73	83	93
4	14	24	34	44	54	64	74	84	94
5	15	25	35	45	55	65	75	85	95
6	16	26	36	46	56	66	76	86	96
7	17	27	37	47	57	67	77	87	97
8	18	28	38	48	58	68	78	88	98
9	19	29	39	49	59	69	79	89	99
10	20	30	40	50	60	70	80	90	100

▲ Seventy-five percent of the students see the reptiles.

Activity Box

Seventy-five percent of the 100 children go to visit the reptiles. How many children go to the reptile house?

More students visit the reptiles than visit the sea lions.

Lunch Time!

The children are hungry. Mr. Santiago decides that it is time for lunch, and they walk to the restaurant. Pedro and Jessica want to share a pizza. Each child will eat **one-half** of the pizza. One-half is equal to 50 percent, or 50%.

The 50% can also be written as a **fraction**. To change a percent to a fraction, remove the % sign. Place the number "over" 100. This means that 50% is $\frac{50}{100}$.

The childrens' pizza is cut into two equal parts. Each part is one-half of the whole. This means they each get one out of two parts, or $\frac{1}{2}$.

Activity Box

Imagine that you are eating lunch. Your sandwich is cut in two equal parts. You eat one of the parts. What percent is that?

1 half | 1 half

50% + 50% = 100%

$$\frac{1}{2} + \frac{1}{2} = 1$$

The whole pizza equals 100%.
Do you think you could you eat
100% of this pizza?

Butterflies

After lunch, the children hurry off to the butterfly **exhibit**. There are 100 butterflies in all! The children see four different kinds of butterflies. Twenty-five percent are Monarchs. Twenty-five percent are Painted Ladies. Twenty-five percent are Cabbage Whites. Twenty-five percent are Giant Swallowtails.

The 100 butterflies are made up of four groups of equal number. Each group is 25%, or $\frac{25}{100}$. We also call this **one-fourth**, because it is one of four equal parts. The $\frac{25}{100}$ can also be written as $\frac{1}{4}$.

Activity Box

There are 100 butterflies at the exhibit, and 25 are Monarchs. What percent are Monarchs?

100%

25%

25%

25%

25%

Monarch Butterfly

Painted Lady
Butterfly

Cabbage White
Butterfly

Giant
Swallowtail
Butterfly

The $\frac{25}{100}$ can also
be written as $\frac{1}{4}$.

15

Camel Rides

At last it is time to visit the camels. This is a very special exhibit. The children get to ride on the animals! Seventy-five percent of the children want to ride the camels. The rest of the group takes a break under a shady tree.

The 75% can also be written as the fraction $\frac{75}{100}$. We can also call this number **three-fourths**. It represents three out of four parts, or $\frac{3}{4}$.

Activity Box

Imagine a round pizza. What if someone took a piece, leaving $\frac{3}{4}$ behind? Draw three–fourths of a pizza. What percent is that?

1	11	21	31	41	51	61	71	81	91
2	12	22	32	42	52	62	72	82	92
3	13	23	33	43	53	63	73	83	93
4	14	24	34	44	54	64	74	84	94
5	15	25	35	45	55	65	75	85	95
6	16	26	36	46	56	66	76	86	96
7	17	27	37	47	57	67	77	87	97
8	18	28	38	48	58	68	78	88	98
9	19	29	39	49	59	69	79	89	99
10	20	30	40	50	60	70	80	90	100

Would you ride the camel?
Are you 100 percent sure?

Estimation

On the way back to the buses, the children go to an ice cream stand. There are two choices of ice cream, vanilla and chocolate. Pedro **estimates** that 75 out of the 100 children will choose chocolate. An estimate is a guess people make using things that they know. Jessica estimates that 25 children will choose chocolate. Who do you think will be closer to the right answer?

Pedro is right! Three out of four children ask for chocolate.

Activity Box

What percent of the children choose chocolate ice cream? What percent choose vanilla?

Three out of four children choose chocolate. Write this number as a percent and a fraction.

Back at School

The children are back at school. They talk about their favorite parts of the trip. They use **tally marks** to keep track of everyone's favorites.

Seventy-five of the children liked the camels the best. This means that 75 percent say that riding the camels was their favorite part. Some children say that they liked the ice cream best. But they are only joking!

Camels	Other
‖‖ ‖‖	‖‖ ‖‖
‖‖ ‖‖	‖‖ ‖‖
‖‖ ‖‖	‖‖
‖‖ ‖‖	
‖‖ ‖‖	
‖‖ ‖‖	
‖‖ ‖‖	
‖‖	

The children take a vote and discover that 100% of the group had fun visiting the zoo!

Activity Box

Ten children out of 100 chose the butterfly exhibit as their favorite part of the trip. What percent is that?

The trip to the zoo was 100 percent fun! You can use the glossary and index on the following pages to think back about it all.

Did you have fun at the zoo?

Yes	No

Glossary

estimates Makes a good guess

exhibit A display of something

fraction Part of a whole

one-fourth ($\frac{1}{4}$) One part of a whole that has been cut into four equal parts

one-half ($\frac{1}{2}$) One part of a whole that has been cut into two equal parts

percent Part of one hundred

symbol In math, a sign or mark that has meaning

tally marks Lines that can be counted to show a number, marked in groups of 5

three-fourths ($\frac{3}{4}$) Three parts of a whole that has been cut into four equal parts

one hundred percent
100%

1	11	21	31	41	51	61	71	81	91
2	12	22	32	42	52	62	72	82	92
3	13	23	33	43	53	63	73	83	93
4	14	24	34	44	54	64	74	84	94
5	15	25	35	45	55	65	75	85	95
6	16	26	36	46	56	66	76	86	96
7	17	27	37	47	57	67	77	87	97
8	18	28	38	48	58	68	78	88	98
9	19	29	39	49	59	69	79	89	99
10	20	30	40	50	60	70	80	90	100

fifty percent
50%

1	11	21	31	41	51	61	71	81	91
2	12	22	32	42	52	62	72	82	92
3	13	23	33	43	53	63	73	83	93
4	14	24	34	44	54	64	74	84	94
5	15	25	35	45	55	65	75	85	95
6	16	26	36	46	56	66	76	86	96
7	17	27	37	47	57	67	77	87	97
8	18	28	38	48	58	68	78	88	98
9	19	29	39	49	59	69	79	89	99
10	20	30	40	50	60	70	80	90	100

$$\frac{1}{2}$$

seventy-five percent
75%

1	11	21	31	41	51	61	71	81	91
2	12	22	32	42	52	62	72	82	92
3	13	23	33	43	53	63	73	83	93
4	14	24	34	44	54	64	74	84	94
5	15	25	35	45	55	65	75	85	95
6	16	26	36	46	56	66	76	86	96
7	17	27	37	47	57	67	77	87	97
8	18	28	38	48	58	68	78	88	98
9	19	29	39	49	59	69	79	89	99
10	20	30	40	50	60	70	80	90	100

$$\frac{3}{4}$$

twenty-five percent
25%

1	11	21	31	41	51	61	71	81	91
2	12	22	32	42	52	62	72	82	92
3	13	23	33	43	53	63	73	83	93
4	14	24	34	44	54	64	74	84	94
5	15	25	35	45	55	65	75	85	95
6	16	26	36	46	56	66	76	86	96
7	17	27	37	47	57	67	77	87	97
8	18	28	38	48	58	68	78	88	98
9	19	29	39	49	59	69	79	89	99
10	20	30	40	50	60	70	80	90	100

$$\frac{1}{4}$$

Index